RESTORATION:

Freedom from Addictions through Jesus Christ-

A Bible Based 12 Principle Manual for Success

Written by Pastor Loren Naffziger with Paula Naffziger

Endorsements

Dr. Loren Naffziger offers passionate and practical insight that will literally set a person free if committed to doing so. In the pages of this timely manual, you will find tools and biblical insight that will set you on a course of passionate connection with Jesus; and Biblical clarity on the supernatural life of freedom available to you. I highly endorse Dr. Loren and Paula Naffziger, and strongly encourage pastors and marketplace leaders, to contact Restoration Ministries. They will assist you in establishing a strategy to bring restoration to the whole person, spirit, soul, and body.

Sincerely,
Pastor Barry Sappington
Senior Pastor – Crosspointe Life Church, La Mesa, CA

***

Pastor Naffziger started Restoration ministries at Foothills Church 19 years ago. I was at Restoration Ranch getting clean at the time and going to Loren's meeting every Monday night. Nine years ago Loren ask me to take the meeting over and it's still going on every week. Loren is well versed in recovery and Restoration Ministries is a wonderful recovery program, very effective.

Sincerely,
Brian Storm-*Executive Director*
Restoration Ranch Ministry

***

My wife Karen and I both attended Restoration Class when Loren and Paula taught it at Foothills Christian Fellowship in El Cajon. As I recall I attended about a year or so. My wife, Karen saw changing results in her life as she attended a short time. I went to the class with my own agendas to deal with but found out the first night that Gods agenda through Restoration Class was far better than mine. As I embraced the class and let go and let God, I to saw incredible result in my life. Restoration Class was not just academic and power point slides; it was very personable as the person of Jesus came through Loren and Paula as they shared it with those who attended.

As I was at Foothills (Christian Church) and (went) on into becoming a pastor myself and seeing and being part of what God is doing with different Christ based recovery homes in San Diego county as well as Riverside county and along with several healing miseries; I have never found a class or program that deals with every life controlling addiction known to mankind like Restoration Class does.

I say all that to say this: My wife and I sincerely endorse Loren and Paula with Restoration Class.

Pastor Mark Baxter
Ramona Vineyard Church

***

For more information, set up the Restoration Ministry at your church, or for personal ministry through web-conferencing or the online course, please contact us at http://bit.ly/restorationministry **or at 619-749-9384.**

Restoration:

Freedom from addictions through Jesus Christ

Written by Pastor Loren Naffziger with Paula Naffziger

ISBN 978-1-61529-160-1

Copyright © 2015 by Loren Benjamin Naffziger

Vision Publishing
1115 D Street
Ramona, CA 92065
1 800 -9- VISION
www.booksbyvision.com

All rights reserved worldwide.

No part of this book may be reproduced in any manner without the written permission of the author except for brief quotations embodied in critical articles or reviews.

Scripture taken from the New American Standard Bible© 1960, 1962, 1963, 1968, 1971, 1972, 1973, 1975, 1977, 1995, by The Lockman Foundation. Used by permission. (www.Lockman.org)

Dedication

We dedicate this manual for success in the battle over addictions and compulsive behaviors to our Lord and Savior Jesus Christ. To Him belongs all the glory and honor! He has sealed our victory in His death and resurrection, which disarmed the enemy of our souls (Colossians 2: 15). Success in the battle for our sanctification comes through the knowledge and surrender of our lives to the Lordship of Jesus Christ.

This work has been a co-labor with the love of my life, Paula, who has stood beside me for nearly 40 years. Together we have been co-laborers with Christ in the work of restoration. For over two decades, we have ministered in the power of the Holy Spirit as God activates the power of His resurrection through the principles found in this manual. We need to acknowledge the loving support of our family, especially our children, Christopher, Shaun, and Jessica. Each of them has grown up in the Lord and served Christ with us. Chris has gone to his eternal reward though he continues to be close to us in our hearts. Our daughter-in-law, Britnie, and son-in-law, Gabriel, are inspirations for all and along with our children; they are raising our grandchildren in the love of Christ.

We want to also lovingly acknowledge our parents, who have been inspirational and supportive of the calling the Lord has on our lives. Our moms, Betty and Ginny continue to show the love of Jesus to all of us. Without them, this work would not have been possible. We extend a special thank you to Betty for making this final part of the journey possible.

RESTORATION…

Freedom from life-controlling addictions or compulsive behaviors through Jesus Christ.

12 BIBLICALLY BASED PRINCIPLES TO OVERCOMING SIN AND BEING RESTORED TO RELATIONSHIPS:

1. **Recognize your sinful nature.**

   I confess I have a life-controlling addiction or compulsive behavior.

   ☦ *For the wages of sin is death, but the free gift of God is eternal life in Christ Jesus our Lord." Romans 6:23*

2. **Confess your sins and be restored to God through Jesus Christ.**

   I confess I need to change my life, but I am unable to do so in my own power.

   ☦ *"…apart from Me you can do nothing." John 15:5*

3. **Seeking forgiveness through repentance.**

   I confess I need forgiveness for the wrongs I have done.

   ☦ *"It is written: `As surely as I live', says the Lord, "every knee will bow before Me; every tongue will confess to God." So then, each one of us shall give an account of himself to God." Romans 14:11-12*

4. **Put off – Put on.**

I confess I need to change the old patterns in my life to new patterns that will please God.

✟ *"YOU SHALL BE HOLY, FOR I AM HOLY." I Peter 1:16*

5. **Life Essentials (Prayer).**

I confess I need to pray in order to hear from and speak to God.

✟ *"Then you will call upon Me and come and pray to Me, and I will listen to you. You will seek Me and find Me when you seek Me with all of your heart. I will be found by you," declares the Lord, "and will bring you back from captivity." Jeremiah 29:12-14*

6. **Life Essentials (Bible Study).**

I confess that I need to study and apply God's Word to my life in order to receive His blessings.

✟ *"Blessed are those who hear the Word of God and obey it." Luke 11:28*

7. **Life Essentials (Worship & Fellowship).**

I confess that I need to worship God in my heart, by my actions, and in fellowship with other believers.

✟ *"God is Spirit and those who worship Him must worship in spirit and truth." John 4:24*

8. **The Holy Spirit in your Life.**

I confess that I need the guidance of the Holy Spirit in my life.

✝ *"But, when He, the Spirit of truth, comes He will guide you into all truth; for He will not speak of His own initiative, but whatever He hears, He will speak; and He will disclose to you what is to come." John 16:13*

9. **Obtain a sober estimate of yourself with the guidance of the Holy Spirit.**

I confess that I need honest help in accurately assessing my life.

✝ *"Man looks at the outward appearance, but the Lord looks at the heart." I Samuel 16:7*

10. **Restoration to the Body of Christ (serving in His Kingdom).**

I confess I need to serve the Lord by serving others, especially those in the Body of Christ.

✝ *"Therefore, as we have opportunity, let us do good to all people, especially to those who belong to the family of believers." Galatians 6:10*

11. **Increasing your faith in Jesus Christ.**

I confess that I need to put my faith in Jesus Christ.

✝ *"I am confident of this: I will see the goodness of the Lord in the land of the living." Psalm 27:13*

12. **A Daily Evaluation of your walk with Jesus Christ.**

I confess that I need to evaluate my daily walk with the Lord in the light of His word.

✝ *"Your Word is a lamp to my feet and a light for my path." Psalm 119:105*

Table of Contents

Introduction	11
Overcoming the Sinful Nature	17
Confession, Repentance, and Freedom through Christ	27
Seeking Forgiveness and Reconciliation	35
Put Off – Put On: Endeavor To Be Holy	43
Life Essential-Prayer	53
Life Essential-Study of the Bible	61
Worship	67
The Holy Spirit in Your Life	73
Obtain a Sober Estimate of Yourself	79
Serving in the Body of Christ	85
Increasing Your Faith in Jesus Christ	91
A Daily Evaluation of My Walk with Jesus Christ	99

Introduction

This publication is the refinement of over 15 years of working in the area of ministry commonly referred to as recovery. As a pastor and scholarly practitioner in the field of education, I have worked with hundreds of individuals, families, and organizations in the battle against alcohol and drug addiction as well as other idols of the heart. It has become clear to me that any type of addiction can become the idol of the heart that separates us from a right relationship with God. Consider the strong warnings throughout the Bible and this succinct position found in Colossians chapter three beginning in verse five:

Therefore, consider the members of your earthly body as dead to immorality, impurity, passion, evil desire, and greed, which amounts to idolatry. For it is because of these things that the wrath of God will come upon the sons of disobedience, and in them you also once walked, when you were living in them.

God has warned us about the consequences of idolatry and in His mercy provided a way of escape through Jesus Christ (Colossians 3:8-11). There are basic Biblical principles that comprise the heart of the Restoration Course, which follows this introduction. The key elements for living a successful Christian life are found in the beginning of the New Testament Church. Specifically, the Book of Acts provides the foundation for this manual and the success is continuing to grow in the second decade of work my wife, Paula, and I are doing in churches.

Life Essentials

In the Book of Acts, chapter two, beginning in verse 42 we find Peter preaching the gospel and people surrendering their lives to Christ. There are four key principles for life in the spirit, or zoe, which refers to a "life real and genuine, devoted to God, blessed" (Thayer & Smith, 1999). The three principles are evident in Acts 2:42: "They were continually devoting themselves to the apostles' teaching and to fellowship, to the breaking of bread and to prayer" (NASB). These principles begin with studying of God's Word, which the apostles were teaching at the time.

The second principle is something that I often refer to as the glue that holds everything together in the believer's life. Just as we see the Trinity operate in unison in the supernatural, Christians operate best in unity through fellowship. Connecting to other believers is the source of Bible study and corporate prayer that keeps one from falling into temptation.

As pastors, we use many analogies to emphasize the need for fellowship. One that stands out for me is the story of the pastor who came to visit a parishioner who had not been attending church for several weeks. The elderly gentleman living in the home graciously invited the pastor in to sit with him by an open fire in the living room. Without saying much in the way of details, the pastor told the member of the church that he was missed and he was there to check on the well-being of one of the congregation. The elderly man said he was fine and felt he did not need others at this time of his life. The pastor looked at him for a moment and turned his gaze to the logs on the fire. One-by-one the pastor separated the logs from each other and what had been a solid flame began to flicker and diminish. The elderly gentleman watched intently and after a few moments told the pastor, he would see him in church next Sunday.

I do not think it is possible to over-emphasize the power of prayer in a believer's life. This principle is the foundation for the powerful life our Savior lived as He walked the earth and it is the principle we read about throughout the Bible. Prayer changes lives, which begins with our own (Mark 11:24) and when we combine the prayers of the saints in harmony it accomplishes more than we can imagine is possible (Revelation 5:8). The illumination of the fourth principle I encourage believers to practice is evident in Acts 2: 47, "praising God and having favor with all the people. And the Lord was adding to their number day by day those who were being saved". Two aspects to praising God are apparent in this passage.

First, the act of praising God was connecting the other principles and it led to favor with the people. Scripture tells us, "Yet You are holy, O You who are enthroned upon the praises of Israel" (Psalm 22:3). The favor of God was also upon these early believers, which comes as God is our focus in life.

The four principles of living a victorious Christian life noted above are present throughout this manual as *Life Essentials*. The second essential element for living a life of victory over an addiction or life controlling behavior is the put off-put on dynamic. As Biblical Counselors, my wife and I have found this truth in Scripture to be powerful as a catalyst for change.

Put off-Put on Principle

The put off-put on principle may appear to be a behavioral approach to life, which has some merit. However, the success of applying this principle comes with the transformation of the mind of the person, who recognizes how they can overcome an addiction or life-controlling behavior (Romans 12:2). It is essential to understand the truth of Ephesians chapter four if you are going to live in freedom; freedom which was the Lord Jesus has purchased for you through His death and resurrection. Consider the following passage in Ephesians, chapter four, starting in verse 17:

So this I say, and affirm together with the Lord, that you walk no longer just as the Gentiles also walk, in the futility of their mind, being darkened in their understanding, excluded from the life of God because of the ignorance that is in them, because of the hardness of their heart; and they, having become callous, have given themselves over to sensuality for the practice of every kind of impurity with greediness. But you did not learn Christ in this way, if indeed you have heard Him and have been taught in Him, just as truth is in Jesus, that, in reference to your former manner of life, you lay aside the old self, which is being corrupted in accordance with the lusts of deceit, and that you be renewed in the spirit of your mind, and put on the new self, which in the likeness of God has been created in righteousness and holiness of the truth.

This passage is clear in stating we have a choice to make as followers of Christ and our minds need to be set on living the new life, which is in the "likeness of God". We can see in verse 22 that we able to put off the old self (and a way of thinking) and put on a new self (verse 24) when our minds are renewed.

Going further into this passage of the book of Ephesians, chapter four, we are given a list of specific behaviors that can be put off and new behaviors that can be put on to bring about the righteousness of Jesus in our lives. This passage is one that some may point to in claiming that Biblical Counseling is founded in Behaviorist Theory, but they are missing the change in thinking I have illuminated above.

Renewing of the Mind

The comparison of the mindset of those who ascribe to the popular Alcohol Anonymous model can be articulated as "sober alcoholic", which pales in comparison to the victorious Christian who is a new creation in Christ (2 Corinthians 5:17). The previous description of the renewal of the mind is essential to using this manual effectively. You must not let popular thinking, unmistakable in phrases like, "Once a drunk, always a drunk" or "My name is …. and I am an alcoholic" become your life fulfilling prophecy. In Christ, you are a new creation that overcomes any addiction or life controlling behavior and becomes the person God has destined you to become.

How to Use this Manual

The design of this manual centers on facilitating the learning of 12 basic principles for living a successful Christian life, which restores you to a right relationship with God through Jesus Christ. If you have not given your life to Jesus, I encourage you to stop right now and pray this simple prayer. "Lord Jesus, I confess that I am a sinner and that I have sinned against God as well as people, even those I love. I believe that you, Jesus, are the Son of God, who died on a cross to pay the price for my sins. I believe that your rose again on the third day and are now seated at the right-hand of God, the Father. I ask you to come into my heart right now and become the Lord of my life. I renounce all detestable practices and ask you to make me clean". If you prayed that prayer, Romans 10 confirms that if we confess Jesus as Lord and believe He was raised from the dead we will be saved. Congratulations on becoming a new creation in Christ and beginning the journey to living in victory over addictions and life-controlling behaviors.

To be able to use this manual you need to know the basics of its design. The design follows some simple principles that can be useful in group work as well as by the individual. First, each of the 12 lessons begins with a confession that should be read aloud. You may be asking, "Why should I read this aloud"? Scripture presents the reason for this public declaration in stating, "He who conceals his transgressions will not prosper, But he who confesses and forsakes them will find compassion" (Proverbs 28:13). Second, there are several areas for you to fill-in blanks, which is a way to check your understanding of the lesson content. Finally, the end of each lesson offers a "Life Application" section, which allows you to practice key principles each week. Blessings upon you as begin the journey of freedom through Christ (John 8:32).

I confess I have had a life-controlling addiction or compulsive behavior.

"For the wages of sin is death, but the free gift of God is eternal life in Christ Jesus our Lord."
Romans 6:23

Overcoming the Sinful Nature

The reason you are struggling with a life-controlling addiction or compulsive behavior is because you have a sin nature that you were born with (Psalm 51:5). The Bible tells us ***"Surely I was sinful at birth, sinful from the time my mother conceived me."*** (Psalm 51:5 NASB). This condition is our inheritance in a fallen world and one we can find victory over in Jesus Christ.

You must recognize your sinful nature (Romans 7:17) so that you can control it through the power of Jesus Christ. You have a heart, will, and mind that is sinful without the sanctifying work of the Holy Spirit. It is your sin nature, which causes you to rebel against God. In fact, part of the definition of sin is rebellion against the holiness and sovereign will of God (Douglas and Tenney, 1989).

☦ *"So now, no longer am I the one doing it, but sin which indwells me." Romans 7:17*

This sinful nature is evident in your thoughts, words, and actions, which reflect your inner heart, will, and mind. Jesus spoke about this inner condition in the Gospel according to Mark (Chapter 7: 21-23) and that inner condition is evident in your relationship with God and in your relationships with other people. We teach children the word "no" early in life to protect them from their choices, which are naïve and often self-centered, which is the manifestation of the sinful nature.

As stated earlier, Jesus explained to us our inner condition when we are not partaking of His holy nature: ***"For from within, out of men's hearts, come evil thoughts, sexual immorality, theft, murder, adultery, greed, malice, deceit, lewdness, envy, slander, arrogance, and folly. All these evils come from inside and make a man unclean." Mark 7:21-23***

The Bible tells us in Romans 7:20: that *"... sin living in me."* is a problem that you must deal with in your everyday life. No one is exempt from this inner condition; therefore, we all must deal with this on a <u>daily</u> basis by putting off sinful desires and putting on righteous ones.

I recognize that my sinful thoughts and behaviors are the result of my _____ nature and I must take responsibility for my thought life and actions. I confess that I have sinned in my _____.

You can deal with this problem by denying yourself, that is, your sinful desires that are contrary to the will of God. This means that you must stop following the things of the world or of the sinful nature and start to follow Jesus Christ. You can do this through the power of the Holy Spirit once you ask Jesus Christ to come into your heart to be your Lord and Savior. You can partake of the holiness of God once you set your mind on Jesus and declare His Lordship over your life. Jesus will set you free if you will accept Him and honestly desire to follow Him.

> ✝ ***"Then He said to them all: "If anybody would come after Me, he must deny himself and take up his cross daily and follow Me." Luke 9:23***

It is critical to your understanding of the sinful nature that once you have given your life to Jesus that you are no longer bound as a slave to sin. It is a <u>choice</u> you make by either giving in to the desires of the sinful nature or being obedient of the leading of Jesus Christ. Sin can no longer bind you unless you give in to the lust of your flesh and deny Jesus Lordship over an area of your life. You have received the victory over every form of evil through the blood of the Lamb (I Corinthians 15:56-58). Be free in Jesus by asking Him to forgive you and by asking Him to take control over that area of your life. Read the following verses aloud and let the Word resonate in your spirit.

☩ *"Don't you know that when you offer yourselves to someone to obey him as slaves, you are slaves to the one whom you obey-whether you are slaves to sin, which leads to death, or to obedience, which leads to righteousness? However, thanks be to God that, though you used to be slaves to sin, you wholeheartedly obeyed the form of teaching to which you were entrusted. You have been set free from sin and have become slaves to righteousness." Romans 6:16-18*

☩ *"The sting of death is sin, and the power of sin is the law; but thanks be to God, who gives us the victory through our Lord Jesus Christ." I Corinthians 15:56-57*

I declare that I have not given _____ (a specific area of my life) over to the Lordship of Jesus Christ. I confess that sin and ask Jesus to take over that area of my life immediately. I declare that I can make a choice to be free from the bondage of _____ through Jesus Christ.

Life-controlling addictions and compulsions are born in your sin nature. When you allow anyone or anything other than God to master your life, you have allowed your sin nature to take control of your life. Jesus Christ said, *"No servant can serve two masters. Either he will hate the one and love the other, or he will be devoted to the one and despise the other. You cannot serve both God and Money."* (Luke 16:13). Jesus tells us in the previous verse that we cannot have more than one master on the throne of our life. (A master is a ruler or lord, who dictates how we live our lives.) Ultimately, man in his fallen state will attempt to control his life through self-indulgence. This sinfulness will also cause a person to attempt to control others, as one is self-consumed with trying to feel good about themselves. Until you place Jesus Christ in **His** rightful position on the throne of your life, you will never experience true blessedness, which is more than mere happiness. Happiness can be a fleeting emotion while blessedness refers to God-given favor in life that indicates His hand being upon you. When you recognize your need for the only true God and humble yourself before Him you receive His blessing.

☩ *"Blessed are the poor in spirit, for theirs is the kingdom of heaven." Matthew 5:3*

God is calling you to turn away from those things or people that you have put before Him in your heart. By repenting (turning away from) of these idols, you can be restored to a relationship with the Living God! By being obedient to the Lord, you can experience the blessing that the Lord has for you, which includes healthy relationships with others.

Relationships can then be restored through your humility and dependence on the Lord. First, you must be restored to your Father in heaven through His Son. This is accomplished by confessing your sins, asking for His forgiveness, and placing Him on the throne of your life. You have the opportunity to start a new life in Jesus. It begins with the recognition of your sin nature, confessing the manifestation of that sin nature (which are your specific sins), asking for God's forgiveness, and placing Jesus on the throne of your life.

✟ *"That if you confess with your mouth, Jesus is Lord, and believe in your heart that God raised Him from the dead, you will be saved. For it is with your heart that you believe and are justified, and it is with your mouth that you confess and are saved." Romans 10:9-10*

Confessing Jesus as Lord begins with publicly declaring that Jesus Christ is your Master, the one whom you will obey and serve. It means that you agree with the Holy Spirit that you have sinned and that you will repent of that sin, which will be evident by your following after Him in every part of your life. The result of the confession will be a new life of righteousness that is attainable because you are a new creation in Christ Jesus (II Corinthians 5:17).

✟ *"Therefore, if anyone is in Christ, he is a new creation; the old has gone, the new has come." II Corinthians 5:17*

I admit that I have had _____ as an idol in my life and I ask God to forgive me now. I declare that I am new in my relationship with _____ by the power of the Living God that empowers me to do what is right in His sight.

Next, you can restore healthy relationships with family and friends through the indwelling presence of the Lord. Jesus enables you to do what you could not do in your own sin nature. You are now able to love others the way the Lord intended you to love others. You must recognize that you will fail to do what is right if you continue to depend on yourself. Rather, you must develop a dependence on God through His Holy Spirit to lead and guide you.

† *Jesus tells us in John 15:5: "…apart from Me you can do nothing."*

I have tried to live without Jesus on the throne of my life. I confess that apart from _____ I cannot do the good I need to do.

Today, you have the opportunity to change the sinful behaviors of your life through the power of the Lord Jesus Christ. Do not let the opportunity slip away; you must seize the moment to be obedient to the call of the Lord. Nobody knows how many opportunities they will have to answer the call of the One whom gives life. There is not a good reason to deny Lordship of your life any longer to Jesus Christ. All the reasons you can think of are veiled attempts to continue to be your own god. Surrender all of your life to the King of Kings for His mercy is great and so is His wrath! Do not harden your heart any more – give it to the One who died for your sins and the One who will bring victory into your life!

† *"for He says, At the acceptable time I listened to you, and on the day of Salvation I helped you; behold, now is the acceptable time", behold now is "The day of Salvation." II Corinthians 6:2*

I confess Jesus Christ as my Lord and Savior. I ask you, Lord Jesus, to take control of my life right now – I surrender all of it to your Lordship. Please forgive me of my sin of_____ and wash me clean again.

Life Application

Merely reading the word of God and failing to apply it to your life is at best foolishness (James 1:22-25). You must apply the Living Word to your life if you intend to truly be a disciple of Jesus Christ (John 14:15). Pray, read, and write out a plan (Proverbs 29:18) for **applying** the word to your life beginning today! Each of four life essentials discussed in the introduction and found in Acts 2 needs to be a part of your life. Keeping a journal of your prayer life, study of God's word, who you are having Christian fellowship with, and how you are applying your learning will begin the process of living a transformed life.

Application of my learning

Christian Fellowship

Bible Study
John Chapters 1-3
John Chapters 4-6
John Chapters 7-9
John Chapters 10-13
John Chapters 13-15
John Chapters 16-19
John Chapters 20-21

Day	Prayer
Sunday	
Monday	
Tuesday	
Wednesday	
Thursday	
Friday	
Saturday	

Confession, Repentance, and Freedom through Christ

> **I confess I need to acknowledge my sins and change my life.**
>
> *"I will confess my transgressions to the Lord – and you forgave the guilt of my sin." Psalm 32:5b*

Confession of your sins means to acknowledge, agree with, declare, and **admit** you are guilty of what you are accused of as the result of inner conviction (pray through Psalm 139:23-24 to get **God's** perspective of your sins). Forgiveness refers to the removal of the penalty Divinely and the deliverance of the sinner from the penalty of death. This forgiveness means that God has removed this sin from your slate (Psalm 103:12) completely – there is no remnant if you have truly asked for forgiveness of a specific sin. Cleansing refers to a removal of the guilt in order to make one spotless from the sin that one has been enslaved to. This cleansing is an absolute purification so that you can begin renewed living in righteousness free from the stain of that specific sin. This promise is for all of those that have accepted the Lord Jesus Christ as their personal Savior and Lord of their lives. Jesus Christ's Lordship in your life is a necessary component for moving forward in life without sinful attachments pulling you into a sinful lifestyle again. Jesus sets you free – you choose to live in it or not live in that freedom.

- *"Search me, O God, and know my heart; test me and know my anxious thoughts. See if there is any offensive way in me, and lead me in the everlasting way." Psalm 139: 23-24*
- *"If we confess our sins, He is faithful and just and will forgive us our sins and purify us from all unrighteousness." I John 1:9*
- *"…as far as the east is from the west, so far has He removed our transgressions from us." Psalm 103:12*

I believe that God's forgiveness is _____. I believe that _____ can show me all of my sins if I ask Him. I ask Him to forgive me for my sins of _____ _____.

If you have confessed Jesus Christ as your Lord and believe He is the Son of God, you have the weapons of spiritual warfare that will bring down strongholds. The battleground you must first engage in is your mind because as you think you are, you are (Proverbs 23:7a). In order to win a victory you must repent of your sins and believe in the power of God to set you free from the slavery of your addictions or compulsions.

Repentance is the process of changing your mind or purpose for the better, which means **you**, must become Spiritually minded. You must put on a Biblical mindset that causes you to think about what is right in God's view and you must put on the attitude that you will live life in accordance to His will – not yours! You must turn away from your sinful ways and turn towards the Lord in your walk of life. You are capable of doing so in the power of the Holy Spirit.

- *"Godly sorrow brings repentance that leads to salvation and leaves no regret, but worldly sorrow brings death." II Corinthians 7:10*
- *"Do not conform any longer to the pattern of this world, but be transformed by the renewing of your mind." Romans 12:2*
- *"Repent, then, and turn to God, so that your sins may be wiped out, that times of refreshing may come from the Lord," Acts 3:19*

I repent on my sin(s) of _____ and ask God to forgive me in the name of Jesus. Godly sorrow brings about _____ whereas worldly sorrow brings _____.

To become Spiritually minded you must live in accordance with the desires' of the Holy Spirit. God enables you to do this when you set your mind on His will and begin to live in obedience to His Word. This process begins with confession of sins and repentance, which demonstrates a desire to change. God wants you to change and return to Him, therefore He promises to enable you to change by His Spirit. Repentance is a gift of God that through His power enables you to change your mind and your way of life to obedience to the Word. You must desire to change and then take the steps necessary to begin a process of sanctification.

- ☦ *"I will give you a new heart and put a new spirit in you; I will remove from you your heart of stone and give you a heart of flesh. And I will put my Spirit in you and move you to follow My decrees and be careful to keep my laws." Ezekiel 36:26-27*
- ☦ *"So I say, live by the Spirit, and you will not gratify the desires of the sinful nature." Galatians 5:16*

I declare that I will live by the _____ and not by the desires of the _____ nature.

The Lord enables you to live a Spiritual life that overcomes all life-controlling addictions or compulsive behaviors. The Word of God, secured through faith in Jesus, sustains this Spiritual life so that you can die to your sinful habits. This Spirit filled life is **Christ** centered and dependent on the weapons of spiritual warfare, which are found in the Word of God. These weapons enable you to break free of the lies of the enemy – you are not the victim of a disease or an alcoholic – you are a new creation in Christ when you surrender to His Lordship over your life. You have victory in the One who has come to set captives free.

- ☦ *"For as a man thinks within himself, so he is." Proverbs 23:7a*

> ✞ *"It is for freedom that Christ has set us free. Stand firm, then, and do not let yourselves be burdened again by a yoke of slavery." Galatians 5:1*

By choosing and then following through with living the Spiritual life, you are freed from your life-controlling addictions or compulsive behaviors. This freedom occurs through reading the Word and then living it out in your life. Your focus must change from yourself to the Lord. This will be evidenced by your love for Him and by your love for others. You cannot remain your own central focus in a Spirit filled life – Jesus Christ must become the central focus in your Spirit filled life.

> ✞ *"Love the Lord your God with all your heart and with all your soul and with all your mind and with all your strength. The second is this: You must love your neighbor as yourself." Mark 12:30-31a*

I confess that I have loved _____ more than Jesus. I repent of that sin, asking Jesus to forgive me and to lead me into the everlasting way.

This restoration to the Sovereign God gives you the power to break the stronghold of any life-controlling addiction or compulsive behavior. You need to put your confidence and trust in Him, so He can guide you into victory. His indwelling presence in you enables you to overcome temptations and live out a life of victory over the sinful nature. His indwelling power will be in your life as long as you choose to love God and be obedient to His commands.

> ✞ *"So do not fear, for I am with you; do not be dismayed, for I am your God. I will strengthen you and help you; I will uphold you with My righteous right hand." Isaiah 41:10*
>
> ✞ *"Not by might nor by power, but by My Spirit, says the Lord Almighty." Zechariah 4:6b*
>
> ✞ *"But the fruit of the Spirit is love, joy, peace, patience, kindness, goodness, faithfulness, gentleness, and self-control." Galatians 5:22-23a*

I confess that I have not asked God to enable me to overcome my sin(s) of _____. I pray that God would forgive me, cleanse me of my unrighteousness, and put His Spirit within me so I can walk in the freedom Jesus brings.

Life Application

Merely reading the word of God and failing to apply it to your life is at best foolishness (James 1:22-25). You must apply the Living Word to your life if you intend to truly be a disciple of Jesus Christ (John 14:15). Pray, read, and write out a plan (Proverbs 29:18) for **applying** the word to your life beginning today! Each of four life essentials discussed in the introduction and found in Acts 2 need to be a part of your life. Keeping a journal of your prayer life, study of God's word, who you are having Christian fellowship with, and how you are applying your learning will begin the process of living a transformed life.

Day	Prayer	Bible Study	Fellowship	Application
Sun.	His strength to obey.	Psalm 139, Acts 2		
Mon.	His strength to obey.	Psalm 139, Acts 3		
Tues.	His strength to obey.	Psalm 139, Galatians 5		

Wed.	His strength to obey.	Psalm 139, Galatians 6		
Thurs.	His strength to obey.	Psalm 139, Psalm 32		
Fri.	His strength to obey.	Psalm 139, II Corinthians 7		

Sat.	His strength to obey.	Psalm 139, Acts 1		

Seeking Forgiveness and Reconciliation

I confess I need forgiveness for the wrongs I have done. "It is written: `As surely as I live', says the Lord, "every knee will bow before Me; every tongue will confess to God." So then, each one of us shall give an account of himself to God." Romans 14:11-12

The reason you need to confess the wrongs you have done to God and others is because **you** need forgiveness. Forgiveness can be defined as the sending away or dismissal of our sins through an atoning sacrifice. This dismissal or release of the due payment of sin was foreshadowed in Old Testament times by the sacrifice of animals and completed in the sacrifice of Jesus Christ in our place. You need forgiveness in order to be reconciled to God and avoid the penalty of your wrongs (sins), which the Bible says is death. Without God's forgiveness you will pay the just penalty for the sins you have committed (which can include sins of omission).

- ✟ *"Surely God will crush the heads of His enemies, the hairy crowns of those that go on in their sins." Psalm 68:21*
- ✟ *"But your iniquities have separated you from your God; your sins have hidden His face from you, so that He will not hear." Isaiah 59:2*
- ✟ *"In Him we have redemption through His blood, the forgiveness of sins, in accordance with the riches of God's grace." Ephesians 1:7*

I confess I have sinned against God by _____. Only the blood of Jesus can redeem my life so that I can have fellowship with God.

By confessing your sins, you can begin with a clean slate before God. Confessing your sins requires the humility and the strength of the Lord working in your life. You can depend upon Him to show you your sins and to be your strength in going before Him and others as you seek forgiveness. Declaring your sins to those that are mature in the Lord provides the basis for you to receive healing and Biblical counseling so you can truly change the course of your life. This confession of sin should lead to a life that is changed to pursuing the righteous of God.

- ✞ *"If we confess our sins, He is faithful and just and will forgive us our sins and purify us from all unrighteousness." I John 1:9*
- ✞ *"I will set out and go back to my father and say to him: Father, I have sinned against heaven and against you." Luke 15:18*
- ✞ *"Humble yourselves before the Lord, and He will lift you up." James 4:10*

I admit that I have sinned against God by _____ and I ask for His forgiveness. I confess I have sinned against _____ and I will ask for their forgiveness as the Lord provides the opportunity.

You must depend on God for reconciliation with all of those you have sinned against. God's forgiveness is immediate and restores us to a right relationship with Him. However, people may be slow to forgive you and refuse to restore their relationship with you. Leave the timing up to God and focus on what you need to do to live a life that is holy and blameless. You can do that because you have the victory over your life-controlling addictions or compulsive behaviors through Jesus Christ. By focusing on Him and being dependent on the leading of the Holy Spirit, you can overcome your past sinful habits and put on **new righteous habits!** This is a process of sanctification as you begin to be obedient to God's Word and the Lord's leading. You must **walk the walk** rather than just talk the talk! **NO EXCUSES!**

- ✞ *"Therefore if anyone is in Christ, he is a new creation; the old has gone, new things has come. All this is from God, who reconciled us to Himself through Christ, and gave us the ministry of reconciliation: that God was reconciling the world to Himself in*

Christ, not counting men's sins against them. And He has committed to us the message of reconciliation." II Corinthians 5:17-19

✞ *"My dear children, I write this to you so that you will not sin. But if anybody does sin, we have one who speaks to the Father in our defense-Jesus Christ, the Righteous One. He is the atoning sacrifice for our sins, and not only ours but also for the whole world." I John 2:1-2*

I rejoice in the knowledge that _____ is the atoning sacrifice for my sins and the sins of everyone else. I declare that I will live my life in obedience to God and I will not let what others do hinder my relationship with Him.

Your walk must be lived out daily independent of what others do and/or say. You must forgive those that sin against you and love them as you have been commanded. This cannot be a conditional love because you have received unconditional love from the Father. That is, you did not earn the love you received from God - He gives it as a gift! You can expect that others will not be obedient to the Word of God, but this does not give you an excuse to sin. You need to develop a lifestyle that moves from merely being forgiven to forgiving others as they may sin against you.

✞ *"Give, and it will be given to you. A good measure, pressed down, shaken together and running over will be poured into your lap. For with the standard of measure you use, it will be measured to you." Luke 6:38*

✞ *"Then Peter came to Jesus and asked, "Lord, how many times will I forgive my brother when he sins? Up to seven times?" Jesus answered, "I tell you, not seven times, but seventy times seven." Matthew 18:21-22*

Just as you reap a blessing for repenting and asking for forgiveness, you can reap a punishment from not forgiving others. You must forgive those that have sinned against you in order to receive forgiveness from God. Just as you need God's continued forgiveness of your sins, you should be willing to forgive someone else more than once or even a few times. God is always patient with us so in the same manner we should be patient with others. Give so that you may receive.

> ✝ *"And when you stand praying, if you hold anything against anyone, forgive him, so that your Father in heaven may forgive you your sins. But if you do not forgive, neither will your Father who is in heaven forgive your sins." Mark 11:25-26*

I recognize that I must _____ others in order to be forgiven. I forgive _____ for the sin of _____ committed against me.

Finally, you must begin to live each day in obedience to God's word. As you mature in your walk with the Lord, you will receive His blessing on the life He has given you through your obedience. Make it a daily habit to seek God's forgiveness and to forgive those that sin against you. As you develop this habit, you will find the mercy you need to succeed in living a blameless life before a holy God.

> ✝ *"Blessed are the merciful, for they will be shown mercy." Matthew 5:7*
> ✝ *"Bear with each other and forgive whatever grievances you may have against one another. Forgive as the Lord forgave you." Colossians 3:13*

I confess that I need to forgive _____ for the offense of _____. I admit that I need forgiveness for the sin of _____. I ask you, Lord Jesus, to forgive me and to give me your heart of forgiveness for others. Amen.

Basic Peacemaking Principles

From *"The Peacemaker"* by Ken Sande

The Four G's:

I Peter 2:12

Glorify God

Get the log out of your own eye

Go and show your brother his fault

Go and be reconciled

The Three Opportunities in Conflict:

I Corinthians 10:31-11:1; Matthew 25:21

Glorify God

Serve others

Grow to be like Christ

The Six "A"'s of Confession:

Proverbs 28:13; Matthew 7:3-5

Admit specifically the sins you committed

Address everyone involved

Avoid if, but, and maybe

Ask for forgiveness

Alter your behavior

Accept the consequences

The Five Steps for Resolving Conflict:

Proverbs 19:11; Matthew 5:23-24, 18:15-20

Overlook minor offenses

Get the log out of your own eye

Talk in private

Take one or two along

Tell it to the church (pastors)

Treat him as an unbeliever

The Four Promises of Forgiveness:

I Corinthians 13:5; Ephesians 4:32

I will not think about the incident.

I will not bring this incident up and use it against you.

I will not talk to others about this incident.

I will not allow this incident to stand between us or hinder our relationship.

The PAUSE Principle of Negotiating:

Philippians 2:3-4; Ecclesiastes 9:16

Prepare

Affirm relationships

Understand interests

Search for creative solutions

Evaluate options objectively and reasonably

Life Application

Merely reading the word of God and failing to apply it to your life is at best foolishness (James 1:22-25). You must apply the Living Word to your life if you intend to truly be a disciple of Jesus Christ (John 14:15). Pray, read, and write out a plan (Proverbs 29:18) for **applying** the word to your life beginning today! Each of four life essentials discussed in the introduction and found in Acts 2 need to be a part of your life. Keeping a journal of your prayer life, study of God's word, who you are having Christian fellowship with, and how you are applying your learning will begin the process of living a transformed life. Pray, read, and fill out this worksheet so that you can begin to applying the Word to your life (Proverbs 29:18).

Day	Who I have sinned against (specific person including God) and the specific sin.	What I did about it! (Prayer, confession, application of Biblical steps, and restoration.)
Sun.		
Mon.		
Tues.		
Wed.		

Thurs.		
Fri.		
Sat.		

Put Off – Put On: Endeavor To Be Holy

I confess I need to change the old habits in my life to new habits that will please God.
"YOU SHALL BE HOLY, FOR I AM HOLY." I Peter 1:16

If you confess that you need to change your life for the better and truthfully want to please God, you can begin to do so today by the power of the Holy Spirit. In order to please God you must put off the sinful nature and put on the new holy nature that is available only through Jesus Christ. You must recognize your sinful habits or patterns of behavior and ask God to help you change those habits or patterns into new ones that please Him. For example, do you always have to smoke a cigarette, joint, or crack when you are faced with a problem? You can turn to the Lord in prayer, His Word in meditation, worship Him for the opportunity to grow, or seek the fellowship of other believers when faced with that same problem in the holiness God calls you to. You must understand what you need to "put off" and what you must "put on" in the place of the old sinful habits and addictions. This understanding will come through hearing and being <u>obedient</u> to the Word of God. It will develop with the practice and discipline of doing what God wants you to do rather than responding the way the world has taught you or the sinful nature pulls you. Put off your idolatry and put on the Christ centered life you are called to.

✞ *"But the Counselor, the Holy Spirit, whom the Father will send in My name, will teach you all things, and will remind you of everything that I have said to you" John 14:26*

> ✝ *"All Scripture is God breathed and is useful for teaching, rebuking, correcting, and training in righteousness, so that the man of God may be thoroughly equipped for every good work." II Timothy 3:16-17*

I confess that I have _____ rather than seek God's way in dealing with the problems I face. I ask God to forgive me for that sin.

You must put your faith in God and His Word, which will give you the wisdom that leads to salvation (II Timothy 3:15). There is a way that seems right to man, but leads to death. You need the provisions of God in your life that will lead you to the abundant life that He has promised. This is not a materially abundant life; rather it is a spiritually abundant life that releases God's power into your life. With His power released into your life - you can slay the Goliaths and cast the mountains out of your path. Ask God to increase your faith in Him so that you can begin to do what He has commanded. He will never leave you or forsake you when you truly seek Him with all of your heart. Until now, you have put your **faith** in a life-controlling addiction or compulsive behavior that has no hope of satisfying what you really need. You need the **life** that is only available through Jesus Christ, which will satisfy your every need.

> ✝ *"There is a way that seems right to man, but in the end it leads to death." Proverbs 14:12*
> ✝ *"The thief comes only to steal and kill and destroy; I have come that they may have life, and have it to the full." John 10:10*
> ✝ *"He replied, 'Blessed rather are those who hear the word of God, and obey it." Luke 11:28*

I admit that I have trusted in _____ rather than in God to overcome the trials in my life. I pray that God would increase my faith and I commit myself to acting on the faith HE has given me to do what HE commands.

By hearing the Word and applying it to your life, you can have the victory over any life-controlling problem. Obeying the Word of God means to follow through so that it becomes a part of you. This obedience will preserve you from harm and the keep you from falling into the schemes of the wicked one. You need to become guarded in following through with the commands the Lord has given us. It is through this that you are sanctified – that is, the Father separates you from the world and your sinful desires in your thoughts, attitudes, and behavior. This process of sanctification frees you from the things of the world and the sinful nature so that they can no longer bind you to repeat the same sinful habits or patterns of behavior.

- ✝ *"Sanctify them by the truth; your word is truth." John 17:17*
- ✝ *"So if the Son shall make you free, you will be free indeed." John 8:36*

Now that you are free to break from the bondage of sin - you need to replace the things in your life that have facilitated this sinfulness. Those things need to be replaced with the provisions of God, which include:

Bible Study – the study and application of the Word.

Worship – Praising Him for who He is, what He has done, and what He will do. Praise Him for the trials – He commands you to rejoice always!

Prayer – communicating with God. Speaking to Him and listening.

Fellowship – spending time with His children in a spirit of family and community, which includes accountability and responsibility.

You need to put off the old things of the sinful nature and put on the new things of God without leaving a void or emptiness. The Bible warns us of the consequences of doing this in the gospel of Luke. The principle is seen in nature by its' abhorrence of a vacuum. Voids will always be filled in our lives as well as they are filled in nature. Something will take the empty spot in your life so you need to fill it with the presence of the Lord!

- ✝ *"When an evil spirit comes out of a man, it goes through arid places seeking rest, and does not find it. Then it says, `I will return to the house I left.' "When it arrives, it finds the house swept clean and put in order. Then it goes and takes seven other spirits more* *wicked than itself, and they go in and live there. And the final condition of that man is worse than the first." Luke 11:24-26*

I accept my responsibility in filling my life. I confess that I have allowed _____ in my life rather the fullness of Jesus. I repent of this and will put on _____ in place of _____.

By understanding this principle and believing that God will provide everything you need to overcome your life-controlling problem you can put the principle of **"put off – put on"** into practice in your life. The Bible gives you several examples of this principle in Ephesians and Colossians. If you will study these examples and apply them to whatever life-controlling addiction and/or compulsive behavior that you have – God will take control of your life.

Put Off	Put On
Falsehood	*Speak the truth…(Ephesians 4:25)*
Stealing	Labor and share with him who has need. (Ephesians 4:28)
Unwholesome words	But only such a word as is good for edification…(Ephesians 4:29)
Bitterness and wrath and anger and clamor and slander…along with all malice.	Kindness to one another, tenderheartedness, and forgiveness. (Ephesians 4:31-32)
Immorality, impurity, passion, evil desire, and greed, which amounts to idolatry. (Colossians 3:5)	
Ignorance and discouragement.	A heart of compassion, kindness, humility, gentleness, patience, forgiveness, and beyond all these things love and unity. (Colossians 3:12-14)
	The Word of Christ dwell within you, with all wisdom, teaching, and admonishment through psalms and hymns…with a thankful heart. (Colossians 3:16)
Anger	Slowness to anger…(Proverbs 15:18)

	Prayer (Matthew 5:44); Blessing (Romans 12:20-21)

You can apply the principle of "put off-put on" to compulsive eating behaviors by putting off the compulsive eating and putting on the study of God's Word or worshiping the Lord. Gambling and sports addictions can be replaced with ministry to your family or reaching out to the lost. In essence, anything that has become a life-controlling problem needs to be replaced with the holiness that God calls you to live in. By utilizing God's provisions, you can put off the sinful addictions and put on the holiness of God. The proof of this change will be manifested in the fruit of your life. Learn to be a fruit inspector in your own garden – let God help you by His Spirit.

☩ *The acts of the sinful nature are obvious: sexual immorality, impurity and debauchery; idolatry and witchcraft; hatred, discord, jealousy, fits of rage, selfish ambition, dissensions, factions and envy; drunkenness, orgies, and the like. I warn you, as I did before, that those that live like this will not inherit the kingdom of God. But the fruit of the Spirit is love, joy, peace, patience, kindness, goodness, faithfulness, gentleness, and self-control." Galatians 5:19-23a*

One of the keys to this process is **thinking** before you act or speak. This process is dependent on taking in the Word, the leading of the Holy Spirit, and then following through in obedience to live a life of holiness. This process begins with holding each thought captive to the obedience of

Christ and that is dependent upon your changing your thinking to line up with the truth of the Word.

- ☦ *"For as a man thinks within himself, so he is." Proverbs 23:7a*
- ☦ *"We demolish arguments and every pretension that sets itself up against the knowledge of God, and we take captive every thought and make it obedient to Christ." II Corinthians 10:5*
- ☦ *"Therefore, I urge you, brothers, in view of God's mercy, to offer your bodies as living sacrifices, holy and pleasing to God – this is your spiritual act of worship. Do not conform any longer to the pattern of this world, but be transformed by the renewing of your mind. Then you will be able to test and approve what God's will is – His good, pleasing and perfect will." Romans 12:1-2*

I declare that I will put off _____ and I declare that I will put on _____ by the power of the Holy Spirit living within me. I am able to do what is right in God's sight by His strength and power.

Life Application

Merely reading the word of God and failing to apply it to your life is at best foolishness (James 1:22-25). You must apply the Living Word to your life if you intend to truly be a disciple of Jesus Christ (John 14:15). Pray, read, and write out a plan (Proverbs 29:18) for applying the word to your life beginning **today!**

Day	Prayer	Bible Study	Fellowship	Application (What I did!)
Sun.	Obey His commands.	Hebrews 11		
Mon.	Obey His commands.	I Peter 1, Galatians 5	Restoration Group	
Tues.	Obey His commands.	Ephesians 4, Colossians 3		
Wed.	Obey His commands.	Romans 10, 11, 12		
Thur.	Obey His commands.	John 8, 10, 17		
Fri.	Obey His commands.	II Corinthians 10		
Sat.	Obey His commands.	Luke 11		

Appendix

I am accepted…

John 1:12 I am God's child.

John 15:15 As a disciple, I am a friend of Jesus Christ.

Romans 5:1 I have been justified.

1 Corinthians 6:17 I am united with the Lord, and I am one with Him in spirit.

1 Corinthians 6:19-20 I have been bought with a price and I belong to God.

1 Corinthians 12:27 I am a member of Christ's body.

Ephesians 1:3-8 I have been chosen by God and adopted as His child.

Colossians 1:13-14 I have been redeemed and forgiven of all my sins.

Colossians 2:9-10 I am complete in Christ.

Hebrews 4:14-16 I have direct access to the throne of grace through Jesus Christ.

I am secure…

Romans 8:1-2 I am free from condemnation.

Romans 8:28 I am assured that God works for my good in all circumstances.

Romans 8:31-39 I am free from any condemnation brought against me and I cannot be separated from the love of God.

2 Corinthians 1:21-22 I have been established, anointed and sealed by God.

Colossians 3:1-4 I am hidden with Christ in God.

Philippians 1:6 I am confident that God will complete the good work He started in me.

Philippians 3:20 I am a citizen of heaven.

2 Timothy 1:7 I have not been given a spirit of fear but of power, love and a sound mind.

1 John 5:18 I am born of God and the evil one cannot touch me.

I am significant…

John 15:5 I am a branch of Jesus Christ, the true vine, and a channel of His life.

John 15:16 I have been chosen and appointed to bear fruit.

1 Corinthians 3:16 I am God's temple.

2 Corinthians 5:17-21 I am a minister of reconciliation for God.

Ephesians 2:6 I am seated with Jesus Christ in the heavenly realm.

Ephesians 2:10 I am God's workmanship.

Ephesians 3:12 I may approach God with freedom and confidence.

Philippians 4:13 I can do all things through Christ, who strengthens me.

Freedom in Christ Ministries, Copyright © 2006-2012

> I confess I need to pray in order to receive God's blessings in my life.
>
> *"Then you will call upon Me and come and pray to Me, and I will listen to you. You will seek Me and find Me when you seek Me with all of your heart. I will be found by you," declares the Lord. "and will bring you back from captivity."*
> *Jeremiah 29:12-14*

Life Essential-Prayer

The reason you need to pray is because only the Lord God can give you a blessed life and part of the access to that blessing is through communication. Communication is the fundamental building block of all relationships including your relationship with the Lord God because it involves heartfelt interaction. Communication with God involves both speaking and listening as its' key components. You must communicate your heart to the Lord and then allow Him to express His heart back to you so you can begin to develop a relationship with Him. A life without this type of relationship with the Lord will be at its' best only partially fulfilling. Prayer is the key access to the full development of a relationship with the Creator of all things (including you).

- ✝ *"O You who hear prayer, to you all men will come." Psalm 65:2*
- ✝ *"…these I will bring to My holy mountain and give them joy in My house of prayer. Their burnt offerings and sacrifices will be accepted on My altar; for My house will be called a house of prayer for all the nations." Isaiah 56:7*

_____, who has promised to hear my prayer has promised me a _____ life, if I will seek Him with _____ of my heart.

Prayer should involve entering into the presence of the Lord with thanksgiving, asking for **His** will to be done, and then listening to His response to you. It is to be done in humility, recognizing that He alone can move in your life to bring down strongholds and break life-controlling addictions and compulsive behaviors. You need to pray so that God's power may be released in your life and in the lives of others (Matthew 6:9-13). This type of prayer involves seeking God's will in your life, recognizing Him for who He is, and for all His goodness. The Holy Spirit will guide you in this type of prayer life and teach you how to pray when you diligently seek the Lord with all of your heart.

- ✞ *"Enter His gates with thanksgiving and His courts with praise; give thanks to Him and praise His name." Psalm 100:4*
- ✞ *"…give thanks in all circumstances, for this is God's will for you in Christ Jesus." I Thessalonians 5:18*
- ✞ *"In the same way, the Spirit helps us in our weakness. We do not know what we ought to pray for, but the Spirit Himself intercedes for us, with groans that words cannot express. And He who searches our hearts knows the mind of the Spirit, because the Spirit intercedes for the saints in accordance with God's will." Romans 8:26-27*

You need to understand that God wants you to develop a relationship with Him. This relationship will be pleasing to the Lord when you pray in the manner He has prescribed. The Bible tells us that the prayers of God's people are like a sweet aroma of incense to Him. This pleases God, who wants to be your strength and your Guardian as you grow in your relationship with Him.

- ✞ *"Ask and it will be given to you; seek and you will find; knock and the door will be opened to you." Matthew 7:7*
- ✞ *"Watch and pray so that you will not fall into temptation. The spirit is willing, but the body is weak." Matthew 26:41*

I confess I have not sought the Lord in _____. I declare that I need to keep asking God for His strength in dealing with _____.

The Lord promises to answer your prayers as He has always answered prayers. God responds to our prayers in accordance with His will and leads us as the Good Shepherd that He is. The Lord God is an ever-present help for those that call upon Him and put their trust in Him.

- ☦ *"The Lord said to him: "I have heard the prayer and plea you have made before me; I have consecrated this temple, which you have built, by putting My name there forever. My eyes and My heart will always be there." I Kings 9:3*
- ☦ *"He will call upon Me, and I will answer him; I will be with him in trouble, I will deliver him and honor him." Psalm 91:15*

There are several heart conditions that cause your specific prayers not to be answered the way you want. I will only briefly mention them here because the good news is that the Lord has given you His way to overcome these conditions. By following the conditions He has set before you, you can be assured of His hearing and answering you. Bible study is paramount to <u>knowing</u> the Lord's will and then <u>praying accordingly</u>.

Disobedience: Deuteronomy 1:45, I Samuel 14:37, 28:6

Secret sin: Psalm 66:18

Indifference: Proverbs 1:28

Neglect of mercy: Proverbs 21:13

Despising the law: Proverbs 28:9

Bloodguiltiness: Isaiah 1:15

Iniquity: Isaiah 59:2, Micah 3:4

Stubbornness: Zechariah 7:13

Instability: James 1:6-7

Self-indulgence: James 4:3

Out of God's Will: II Corinthians 12:8

Wife neglect: I Peter 3:7

I confess that _____ has been a sin in my life and has hindered my prayer life.

Praying according to the Lord's commands gives, you access to the blessing He has for you. He demands that you approach His throne humbly, seeking after Him with all of your heart, and believing that He will answer your prayers in accordance with His Will. You must live a righteous life that is obedient to His Word in order to receive the fullness of His blessings.

- ☦ *"if My people, who are called by My name, will humble themselves and pray and seek my face and turn from their wicked ways, then I will hear from heaven and will forgive their sin and will heal their land." II Chronicles 7:14*
- ☦ *"... and receive from Him anything we ask, because we obey His commands and do what pleases Him." I John 3:22*
- ☦ *"This is the confidence we have in approaching God: that if we ask anything according to His will, He hears us." I John 5:14*

_____ is the key heart condition before I pray that opens the gates of heaven for an outpouring of God's healing. My _____ to His commands then will lead to answered prayer. I confess I need to pray according to God's will in _____ (specific area of my life).

In summary, to have a relationship with the Lord you must communicate with Him through prayer. This exchange can be done in quiet times alone with Him and in corporate times of prayer with Him. In either setting, you must be open to seriously having an interaction of the heart so that you can fully develop the relationship. Actively seeking to know the Lord will lead to His blessing if it is coupled with obedience to His word and leading. This activation of the Lord God's blessing involves a daily interaction of communication where you spend time speaking and listening to the Lord. By developing this relationship, you will begin to be able to discern the true voice of God and follow His leading into a blessed life.

- ☦ *"My sheep listen to My voice; I know them, and they follow Me." John 10:27*

Life Application

Merely reading the word of God and failing to apply it to your life is at best foolishness (James 1:22-25). You must apply the Living Word to your life if you intend to truly be a disciple of Jesus Christ (John 14:15). Pray, read, and write out a plan (Proverbs 29:18) for **applying** the word to your life beginning today! Each of four life essentials discussed in the introduction and found in Acts 2 needs to be a part of your life. Keeping a journal of your prayer life, study of God's word, who you are having Christian fellowship with, and how you are applying your learning will begin the process of living a transformed life.

Day	Prayer	Bible Study	Fellowship	Application (What I did!)
Sun.	To know Him.	Psalm 27, 91 Matthew 5-7		
Mon.	To know Him.	Psalm 27, 91 Hebrews 3-4	Restoration Group	
Tues.	To know Him.	Psalm 27, 91 I John 1		

Wed.	To know Him.	Psalm 27, 91 I John 2		
Thur.	To know Him.	Psalm 27, 91 I John 3		
Fri.	To know Him.	Psalm 27, 91 I John 4		

Sat.	To know Him.	Psalm 27, 91 I John 5		

Life Essential-Study of the Bible

I confess that I need to study and apply God's Word to my life.

"Blessed are those who hear the Word of God and obey it." Luke 11:28

One of the reasons you need to study the Word is because of the **blessing** that comes from the **study** and **obedience** of the Word of Life. You have a life with a bright future with promises of prosperity as God works to bring about His will into your life through your obedience to Him. Careful study of the Bible combined with a desire to please God equips you for the life He has created you for. The life God promises those that are obedient to Him is a life filled with His presence and an equipping to do the work He has called you to. When you become obedient to the Word of God, you will know true satisfaction and fulfillment in life. Through careful study and a true heart's desire, you will become obedient to all that God requires of you. He has sent His Spirit to guide you as you study and apply God's word to your life.

Some of His blessings for those that are **obedient**:

- ✝ *"Lord, to whom shall we go? You have the words of eternal life." John 6:68*
- ✝ *"My mother and brothers are those who hear God's word and put it into practice." Luke 8:21*

> ✝ *"If you remain in Me and My words remain in you, ask whatever you wish, and it will be given you." John 15:7*

God's blessings for obedience to His Word include a _____ life, adoption into _____ family, and _____ what I ask for. I understand my (specific sin) _____ has separated me from God's blessing.

You need to **study** the Word because you are commanded to do so in the Scriptures (II Timothy 2:15). By being obedient to this command, you will know the Word that leads to salvation and God will release His power into the life He has given you. You need the intake of the Word, as it is food for the Christian soul and a great source of inspiration for a life in Christ. This type of life opens the doors for growth in the knowledge of the Lord and in your relationship with Him. The study of God's word will lead you into that type of relationship with Him because you will know His will and purpose in the things you experience in life. Your relationship with Jesus can be one in which you know Him and are able to relate to Him on the basis of this deep knowledge.

> ✝ *"Do your best to present yourself to God as one approved, a workman who does not need to be ashamed and who correctly handles the word of truth." II Timothy 2:15*
>
> ✝ *"All Scripture is God-breathed and is useful for teaching, rebuking, correcting and training in righteousness, so that the man of God may be thoroughly equipped for every good work." II Timothy 3:16-17*

I need to study God's _____ because I am _____ to do so and studying brings about a _____ that develops my relationship with Jesus. I acknowledge that my _____ (specific sin) has strained my relationship with Jesus.

Through the careful study of the Bible, you can begin to discern the truth from error or lies. The first place you need to apply this discernment is in your own life – not in everyone else's. Your heart will always try to deceive you, but diligent study of the Word will equip you to detect the deception and correct the error so that you can live in **obedience** to the Words of Christ. Again, God gives us the Holy Spirit to lead us and guide us into the truth to live a life that is pleasing to the One whom created us, who never leaves us without the means to live that life. Careful study and application of the Word coupled with the Lord's help will enable us to be obedient to Him.

- ☦ *"For the word of God is living and active and sharper than any two-edged sword, and piercing as far as the division of soul and spirit, of both joints and marrow, and able to judge the thoughts and intentions of the heart." Hebrews 4:12*
- ☦ *"The precepts of the Lord are right, giving joy to the heart. The commands of the Lord are radiant, giving light to the eyes." Psalm 19:8*

I can keep my life pure by being _____ to the word of God. I recognize that I have not been obedient to God's Word when I _____ (specific act of disobedience or sin).

The Bible is the standard by which every life will be judged. This does not apply just to us who have the Word in book form, but also to each of us as God has given each of us His Word (or law) in our hearts. God sent His Spirit into the world to convict the world of sin and to lead everyone into the everlasting way if they would be obedient to His law, which has been written in every human heart. His standard has not and will not change over time; rather it will stand eternally as the basis for all lives to be judged. Finally, as we live in a war for our lives God has given us His Word as a weapon by which we can conquer all evil. As our Lord Jesus demonstrated, we can overcome sin with the skilled application of the Word, which allows us to draw nearer to Him as well.

- ☦ *"The grass withers and the flowers fall, but the Word of our God stands forever." Isaiah 40:8*
- ☦ *"For it is not those who hear the law who are righteous in God's sight, but it is those who obey the law who will be declared righteous. (Indeed, when Gentiles, who do not have the law, do by nature things required by the law, they are a law for themselves, even though they do not have the law, since they show that the requirements of the law are written on their hearts, their consciences also bearing witness, and their thoughts*

now accusing, now even defending them.) This will take place on the day when God will judge men's secrets through Christ Jesus, as my gospel declares." Romans 2: 13-16

The Word of God is the offensive weapon in your arsenal that enables you to accurately and quickly combat the lies of the enemy in your life. By knowing and understanding the Bible, you can destroy the lies the enemy may try to speak into your life and break down the barriers that have held you captive to a false god. Careful study and application will allow you to speak God's truth into your life and the lives of others as the Lord leads you. Furthermore, as you develop skill in the use of your spiritual sword you will be able to be used mightily by God to attack the enemy in other arenas. Similarly, the knowledge of the Bible will enable you to develop a knowledge and understanding of who the Lord Jesus Christ is so that your personal relationship with Him may grow.

- *"Take the helmet of salvation and the sword of the Spirit, which is the Word of God." Ephesians 6:17*
- *"You diligently study the Scriptures because you think that by them you possess eternal life. These are the Scriptures that testify about Me, yet you refuse to come to Me to have life." John 5:39-40*

God's word is written on our _____ and is the eternal _____ by which all people will be judged.

I know that I can study the _____, be _____ to what it says, and I know that I will receive God's _____ for doing so.

Life Application

	Prayer	Bible Study	Worship	Fellowship
Sun.	I will be obedient to your Word, my God.	Romans 1-2		
Mon.	I will be obedient to your Word, my God.	Psalm 119		
Tues.	I will be obedient to your Word, my God.	John 1		
Wed.	I will be obedient to your Word, my God.	John 2		
Thurs.	I will be obedient to your Word, my God.	John 3		
Fri.	I will be obedient to your Word, my God.	John 4		
Sat.	I will be obedient to your Word, my God.	John 5		

Appendix

Learning enhancements for studying the Word of God.

The Master Christian Library – a computer program with a wealth of resources including some of the items listed below.

Commentary – (Matthew Henry's) a discussion of each passage of Scripture.

Nave's Topical Bible – nearly 1000 topics in the Bible are defined with Scripture references for a thorough study of each area.

NIV Compact Dictionary of the Bible – a dictionary of the Hebrew and Greek words as translated by the NIV Bible.

Strong's Concordance of the Bible – a reference guide to locate words in the Bible.

Vine's Expository Dictionary – a thorough study of key Greek words with their original language translated for a richer understanding.

I confess that I need to worship God by my words as well as by my actions and I need to fellowship with other believers. *"God is spirit, and those who worship Him must worship in spirit and truth." John 4:24*

Worship

You need to acknowledge God because you were created by Him and for Him. God created you with a need to worship, which will be evident in your life, either by a relationship with Him or in a relationship with an idol. When you are consumed with a life-controlling addiction or compulsive behavior, you are worshipping a false god or idol. This will always leave you empty and seeking a relationship with the One whom you were created to worship. You must fill your heart and spirit with praise to the Lord because of who He is, what He has done, and what He promises to do. Only by worshipping the Living God, the only real God, will you be satisfied and filled with true life. The life that is available only through Jesus and is truly satisfying is a life filled with worship for the Lord.

- ☩ *"Turn to Me and be saved, all you ends of the earth; for I am God, and there is no other." Isaiah 45:22*
- ☩ *"My soul longed and even yearned for the courts of the Lord; my heart and my flesh sing for joy to the living God." Psalm 84:2*
- ☩ *"For by Him all things were created, both in the heavens and on the earth, visible and invisible, whether thrones or dominions or rulers or authorities – all things have been created by Him and for Him." Colossians 1:16*

I need to worship God because I was _____ by Him and for _____.

There are several Greek words that are translated as worship in the English language. W.E. Vine in **"Vine's Expository Dictionary of Old & New Testament Words"** (Thomas Nelson, Inc., 1997; pg. 1248) summarizes the verbs translated to mean worship with this interesting statement:

> The worship of God is nowhere defined in scripture. A consideration of the above verbs shows that it is not confined to praise; broadly it may be regarded as the direct acknowledgement to God, of His nature, attributes, ways and claims, whether by the outgoing of the heart in praise and thanksgiving or by the deed done in such acknowledgement.

Scripture provides you with a culmination of all the aspects that go into true worship (John 4:24). It is when you truly have a heart, mind, soul, and spirit that worship God that you can enter into true worship. In this condition, you can serve the Lord in a manner that truly reflects an attitude of worship.

Now, you may be asking what does a true worshiper of God look like. What are some of the characteristics that make up a worshiper of the Lord? How do you come to the place in your life where you truly worship God? Scripture provides you with a picture of a true worshiper of the Lord in the following passages. You need to remember who the Lord is, what He has done, and what He will do. Then you must worship Him for who He is, what He has done, and what He will do!

- ☦ *"But an hour is coming, and now is, when true worshipers shall worship the Father in spirit and truth; for such people the Father seeks to be His worshipers." John 4:23*
- ☦ *"Ascribe to the Lord the glory due His name; worship the Lord in the splendor of His holiness." Psalm 29:2*

I should worship God in _____ and in _____ because of the _____ due to His name.

By worshipping the Lord and by being in fellowship with others you can develop a **lifestyle** of worship. This is one of the many benefits of fellowship, which you gain from a relationship with other disciples of Jesus Christ. Several other benefits are listed in the text below. You must remember that you are not only created to worship the Lord, but to be in fellowship with others (John 17:21-23). You need the encouragement and stimulation of others to further your walk with the Lord, which includes a lifestyle of worship in fellowship with other believers (Hebrews 10:23-25).

- ☦ *"that all of them may be one, Father, just as You are in Me and I am in You. May they also be in Us so that the world may believe that You have sent Me. I have given them the glory that You gave Me, that they may be one as We are One; I in them and You in Me. May they be brought to complete unity to let the world know that You sent Me and have loved them even as You have loved Me." John 17:21-23*
- ☦ *"Let us hold fast the confession of our hope without wavering, for He who promised is faithful; and let us consider how to stimulate one another to love and good deeds, not forsaking our own assembling together, as is the habit of some, but encouraging one another; and all the more, as you see the day drawing near." Hebrews 10:23-25*

Fellowship should include _____ others and _____ just as Jesus was _____ with the Father.

Becoming a true worshipper of God is tied into fellowship with other believers (Luke 24:52-53). You will mature in all your Christian activities as you worship and serve others in fellowship. In this setting, the gifting the Lord has given you will be developed for His glory. God has called us to live in a body of fellowship that continues to mature and develop for His purposes to be accomplished in the lives of everyone.

- *"Then they worshiped Him and returned to Jerusalem with great joy. And they stayed continually at the temple, praising God." Luke 24:52-53*
- *"Each one should use whatever gift he has received to serve others, faithfully administering God's grace in its various forms." I Peter 4:10*
- *"Therefore encourage one another and build each other up, just as in fact you are doing." I Thessalonians 5:11*

There is strength in the unity of believers that is beyond human reasoning. God's power released by the fellowship of His people is exponential as unity multiplies the release of His power. This power is focused by the gathering of believers that are acting in unity for the common good. You are a part of that power as you contribute to the fellowship of believers in Christ. We can unlock God's Kingdom power as we gather together in unity while seeking God's will and praising Him for who He is.

- *"Five of you will chase a hundred, and a hundred of you will chase ten thousand, and your enemies will fall by the sword before you." Leviticus 26:8*
- *"Again, I tell you that if two of you on earth agree about anything you ask for, it will be done for you by My Father in heaven." Matthew 18:19*

I recognize that I have put _____ before worshipping God. I will commit myself to fellowship at _____ because I know I am commanded to do so and because I want to see God's power.

Life Application

Study the following Scriptures and respond to them. Pray, read through the Scriptures, ask God to reveal to you how He would have you **apply** them to your life, and then respond!

Emotional strength and encouragement:	Hebrews 3:13
Friendship:	Proverbs 27:9
Accountability and counsel:	Proverbs 27:17
Love and acceptance:	Proverbs 27:6
Help in times of trouble:	Proverbs 17:17
Prayer:	Matthew 18:19
Opportunity to give of ourselves:	John 13:35
Experience the gifts of God and give:	Ephesians 4:15-16

Hebrews 3:13
Proverbs 27:9
Proverbs 27:17
Proverbs 27:6
Proverbs 17:17

Matthew 18:19	
John 13:35	
Ephesians 4:15-16	

Day	Prayer life	Christian Fellowship
Sunday		
Monday		
Tuesday		
Wednesday		
Thursday		
Friday		
Saturday		

The Holy Spirit in Your Life

I confess that I need the Holy Spirit to guide me into a holy lifestyle.
"And the disciples were continually filled with joy and with the Holy Spirit."
Acts 13:52

There are a number of reasons why you need the Holy Spirit in your life. To understand some of them you can look at some of the roles or attributes of the Holy Spirit as Scripture shows us in Isaiah 11:2. The early church disciples needed the continually infilling presence of the Holy Spirit to lead them and guide them into the truth of how they were to live. Today, we all need that same leading and guidance to live a life full of joy and fulfillment in the Lord Jesus Christ. His presence in your life will give you the strength and power to conquer any life-controlling addiction or compulsive behavior. Beyond that, the Holy Spirit in your life coupled with your obedience will guide you into a satisfying life that glorifies the Lord Jesus Christ.

- *"The Spirit of the Lord will rest on Him – the Spirit of wisdom and of understanding, the Spirit of counsel and of power, the Spirit of knowledge and of the fear of the Lord - ... Isaiah 11:2*
- *"...do not walk according to the flesh, but according to the Spirit. For those who are according to the flesh set their minds on the flesh, but those that who are according to the Spirit, the things of the Spirit. For the mind set on the flesh is death, but the mind set on the Spirit is life and peace, ..." Romans 8:4b-6*

To live a life of freedom I need to know the _____ of the Holy Spirit in my life. I acknowledge that I have not set my mind on the Spirit of God in _____ (an area of your life).

When you confess your need for the Lord, repent, and allow Him to lead you, He promises to change you. All believers receive the Holy Spirit and by following His guidance **all** are able to live overcoming lives. You must let Him **guide** you on the path that He has for you. The Spirit of **power** enables you to say **no** to the sinful desires of the flesh and be obedient to the commands of God. Only true believers will know the Holy Spirit in the fullness Christ has intended for us to know Him. This Spirit of **knowledge** will keep us on the right path when we choose to follow His leading and guidance.

> ✞ *"Peter replied, "Repent and be baptized every one of you, in the name of Jesus Christ for the forgiveness of sins. And you will receive the gift of the Holy Spirit." Acts 2:38*
>
> ✞ *"…that is the Spirit of truth, whom the world cannot receive, because it does not know Him, but you know Him because He abides with you, and will be in you." John 14:17*

The fullness of the Holy Spirit is for those that accept _____ as their personal Savior. I confess I have trusted _____ for the truth rather than the Spirit of all Truth.

The Holy Spirit is your **Helper** (John 16:7), who comes along side you to teach you the things you need to know. He uses the **Word** to teach you by bringing to remembrance the things you should say and do (John 14:26). When you decide to allow the Holy Spirit to work in your life He will also convict you of sin (John 16:8) and then restore you to life with your confession and repentance (Romans 8:11). You must trust in the Holy Spirit's assurance that you belong to Jesus (Romans 8:16) and never allow your walk to quench His power in your life (I Thessalonians 5:19).

> ✞ *"But the Helper, the Holy Spirit, whom the Father will send in My name, He will teach you all things, and bring to remembrance all that I said to you." John 14:26*

- *"And He, when He comes, will convict the world concerning sin, and righteousness, and judgment;" John 16:8*
- *"Do not quench the Spirit;" I Thessalonians 5:19*

I declare and renounce my _____ (specific sin), which quenched the Holy Spirit in my life. The Holy Spirit was sent to convict the world of _____. I can surely expect Him to convict me as a believer when I ask and listen.

The Holy Spirit assists you in prayer (Romans 8:26-27), which enables you to receive the anointing of God (I John 2:20). This anointing is communication in which you are taught the truth, which only comes from God. When you walk in this anointing, He will speak to you, which will show you the way to go (Isaiah 30:21). Then, you will know the power of the Lord as you continue to be filled with the baptism of the Holy Spirit (Acts 13:52). This power, which can only come from God (Acts 4:31; II Timothy 1:7), will enable you to conquer any life-controlling addiction or compulsive behavior.

- *"And in the same way the Spirit also helps our weakness; for we do not know how to pray as we should, but the Spirit Himself intercedes for us with groanings too deep for words; and He who searches the hearts knows what the mind of the Spirit is, because He intercedes for the saints according to the will of God." Romans 8:26-27*
- *"And your ears will hear a word behind you, "This is the way, walk in it," whenever you turn to the right or to the left." Isaiah 30:21*
- *"For God has not given us a spirit of timidity, but of power and love and discipline." II Timothy 1:7*

I understand that God has given me a spirit of _____ and _____ and _____. I declare that by the strength of the Lord I can overcome _____ (specific sin).

The power of the Holy Spirit in your life should be evident. The evidence will come from your daily walk with Him, which is manifested in the fruit of your life (Galatians 5:22-23).

Examine the fruit in your life with the help of the Holy Spirit and make the changes necessary for you to walk in His power.

- ✞ *"I am going to send you what my Father has promised; but stay in the city until you have been clothed with power from on high." Luke 24:49*
- ✞ *"But the fruit of the Spirit is love, joy, peace, patience, kindness, goodness, faithfulness, gentleness, self-control; against such things there is no law." Galatians 5:22-23*
- ✞ *"And the disciples were continually filled with joy and with the Holy Spirit." Acts 13:52*

Just as a bad spot on an apple is evident of a problem, as I inspect the fruit of my life, I confess that _____ is evident as sin. I declare that I desire good fruit in _____ (specific area) and I will ask the Holy Spirit to heal this area of my life.

Life Application

Merely reading the word of God and failing to apply it to your life is at best foolishness (James 1:22-25). You must apply the Living Word to your life if you intend to truly be a disciple of Jesus Christ (John 14:15). Pray, read, and write out a plan (Proverbs 29:18) for **applying** the word to your life beginning today! Each of four life essentials discussed in the introduction and found in Acts 2 need to be a part of your life. Keeping a journal of your prayer life, study of God's word, whom you are having Christian fellowship with and how you are applying your learning will begin the process of living a transformed life.

Below are several chapters of Scripture that you may read and apply to your life. These Scriptures deal specifically with the Holy Spirit and who He is. Pray and then apply this to your life. The previous lessons also contain Scripture that may be applied to your life. What are you waiting for? May the Lord richly bless you in your effort to please Him!

Day	Scripture	Application to my life
Sun.	John 14	
Mon.	John 15	
Tues.	John 16	
Wed.	Acts 1	

Thurs.	Acts 2	
Fri.	Acts 19	
Sat.	I Cor. 2	

Prayer:

___

___

___

Worship:

___

___

___

Fellowship:

___

___

___

Obtain a Sober Estimate of Yourself

I confess that I need honest help to assess my life.
"Man looks at the outward appearance, but the Lord looks at the heart." *I Samuel 16:7*

You must make a decision to inventory your life with God's help. You cannot make an honest evaluation without His help because your sin nature deceives you. Only God can honestly and accurately assess your heart, which will show you where your life is right now. If you will write out what the Lord shows you as sins you can begin to confess, repent, and work at changing your life with the guidance of the Holy Spirit. A **written inventory** will allow you to obtain a sober estimate of yourself, which will then allow you to correct those things that you do have control over (attitudes, character, and **choices**). You must ask the Lord for His guidance in finding all those things that are hurtful to others and yourself. Since you cannot trust your own understanding you must have God search your heart and reveal its' ways to you. Heart in the Hebrew is "Leb", which includes the inner nature of man. That inner nature encompasses the human mind, will, and emotion intertwined with the spirit. The word "try" in the verse below refers to an examination in order to search out and **purify**. The word means to investigate in order to determine the essential qualities of the object, which in the case below would be the heart.

✞ *"The heart is more deceitful than all else. And is desperately sick; Who can understand it? I, the Lord, search the heart, I test the mind, Even to give each man according to his ways, according to the results of his deeds." Jeremiah 17:9-10*

✝ *"For in his own eyes he flatters himself too much to detect or hate his sin." Psalm 36:2*

✝ *"There is none righteous, not even one;" Romans 3:10*

Only _____ can truly know my heart because my heart will deceive me in my sin. I confess I have trusted _____ to show me what my sins are.

What you need to do with God's help.

Once the Lord has revealed your heart, you must decide to repent of those sins in your life that are holding you back from a relationship with God and others. The Lord will often use <u>others</u> to speak to you of the error of your way and to help illuminate the path you are to walk. You must make a **conscious** effort to change from sinful patterns and ways to a true walk with the Lord. This is possible because the Lord promises to support you when you give **<u>all</u>** of your heart over to Him. You must also ask the Lord to show you the idols of your heart. An idol can be a person or a thing that has become a god to you. Idolatry is defined as an object of worship or something that is in reality vain or empty. It is someone or something that you honor, trust, serve, or go to as a replacement for the Lord. You must ask God to forgive you and repent from (turn away from and change your thinking towards) the idol(s) in your life so that you can enjoy God's blessing in your life.

✝ *"Son of man, these men have set up idols in their hearts and put wicked stumbling blocks before their faces. Should I let them inquire of Me at all? ... This is what the Sovereign Lord says: Repent! Turn from your idols and renounce all your detestable practices!" Ezekiel 14:3, 6*

✝ *"Search me, O God, and know my heart; Try me and know my anxious thoughts; And see if there is any hurtful way in me, And lead me in the everlasting way." Psalm 139:23-24*

I confess that I have served the false god of _____, which has been an idol in my heart. I ask you, Lord Jesus to forgive me and make me clean again right now.

God's provision for our life.

In addition to being created for the Lord, you can only escape His judgment by the confession of your sins, repentance, and following His leading in your life. The process starts with knowing and repenting of your specific sins, which the Lord will show you when asked. After you begin this process, the Lord will provide the help you need to follow His path. He does this through the leading of the Holy Spirit, His Word, prayer, worship, and fellowship. Only by having, these essentials in your life can you; stay on the righteous path the Lord would have you walk. Jesus promised us His peace and strength when we come to Him in submission to His Lordship.

- ✞ *"Come to Me, all who are weary and heavy-laden, and I will give you rest. Take My yoke upon you, and learn from Me, for I am gentle and humble in heart, and you shall find rest for your souls. For My yoke is easy, and My load is light." Matthew 11:28-30*
- ✞ *"But the Helper, the Holy Spirit, whom the Father will send in My name, He will teach you all things, and bring to your remembrance all that I said to you." John 14:26*

_____ has promised that His burden is light when I come to Him. I admit that I have kept the burden of _____ and not given it to Jesus.

With the help of the Lord, you have the strength and ability to do all that God requires of you. You must make the effort to **write out a list** of <u>how</u> you have sinned and against whom you have sinned. Recognize that when you have sinned against God's creation you have sinned against God Himself. Confess that sin and then go forward in your efforts to be reconciled to others. You must make a conscious effort to put off the old self with its' sinful attitudes, choices, and character and put on the new self, which is being transformed into the image of Jesus Christ. The Lord has promised to support you as you decide to do so. He will be your strength and helper as you endeavor to be holy in Jesus name.

✟ *"I acknowledged my sin to You and did not cover up my iniquity. I said, "I will confess my transgressions to the Lord -and You forgave the guilt of my sin." Psalm 32:5*

✟ *"Therefore, my dear friends, as you have always obeyed-not only in my presence, but now much more in my absence-continue to work out your salvation with fear and trembling, for it is God who works in you to will and to act according to His good purpose." Philippians 2:12-13*

✟ *"Blessed are those who hunger and thirst for righteousness, for they will be satisfied." Matthew 5:6*

God promises to _____ my sin of _____ when I confess it and ask for His forgiveness. God promises His blessings for those that _____ and _____ for righteousness.

Life Application

Merely reading the word of God and failing to apply it to your life is at best foolishness (James 1:22-25). You must apply the Living Word to your life if you intend to truly be a disciple of Jesus Christ (John 14:15). Pray, read, and write out a plan (Proverbs 29:18) for applying the Word to your life beginning today!

Day	My sinful thoughts, attitudes, and behaviors. Matthew 15:19	What I did about it! (Confession, Bible Study, prayer, worship, and/or fellowship).
Sun.		
Mon.		
Tues.		
Wed.		
Thur.		
Fri.		
Sat.		

Prayer:

_____
_____
_____
_____
_____
_____

Worship:

_____
_____
_____
_____
_____

Fellowship:

_____
_____
_____
_____
_____
_____

Serving in the Body of Christ

I confess I need to serve the Lord by serving others, especially those in the Body of Christ.

✝ *"Therefore, as we have opportunity, let us do good to all people, especially to those who belong to the family of believers." Galatians 6:10*

You should want to serve the Lord by serving others because the Lord has commanded you to do so (John 13:14) and because serving brings His blessing into your life (Psalm 119:2). Additionally, service to others is indicative of the love you have for God because the love you show to others is an indication of the love you have for God. To understand what it means to serve let us first look at the definition of service. To "serve" is defined as being a servant, attendant, to wait upon, to minister, or to render service to. In the Greek language, the words translated as serve or service are verbs – in other words – there is an **action** that needs to take place! Be assured that God is always looking at your heart and your actions illuminate your hearts' condition (Luke 6:45). Your life is the manifested condition of your heart, which can be changed through obedience to the Lord. God has called you to live a life of sacrificial service just as the Lord Jesus did in dying on a cross in your place. Jesus said very clearly that He had come to be a servant and then showed you the sincerity of His heart by His actions!

- *"just as the Son of Man did not come to be served, but to serve, and to give His life as a ransom for many." Matthew 20:28*
- *"No one has ever seen God; but if we love one another, God lives in us and His love is made complete in us." I John 4:12*

Service is an _____ that provides evidence of my _____ condition. If I truly love God, I must show _____ to others. I confess that I have served _____ rather than God.

God expects us to serve Him by serving others and in fact, service is an act of worship to the Lord. Therefore, serve others with an attitude of worship - not with an attitude of disgust or self-pity. Offer yourself as a pleasing sacrifice to God in your service, which will bring about God's blessing and joy in your life. This will accomplish far more than any self-serving acts or a "poor me" attitude. Serve the Lord as an act of worship to Him for His glory! Denounce all the other gods you have served and serve the King of Kings alone!

- *"Then Jesus said to him, "Be gone, Satan! For it is written, YOU SHALL WORSHIP THE LORD YOUR GOD, AND SERVE HIM ONLY." Matthew 4:10*
- *"Therefore, I urge you, brothers, in view of God's mercy, to offer your bodies as living sacrifices, holy and pleasing to God – this is your spiritual act of worship." Romans 12:1*

I confess I have served _____ rather than the King of Kings. I commit myself to serving God as an act of _____.

There are several keys to successful service to others through God that need to be utilized for His glory. By the application of these keys, you can serve the Lord with His strength and with His joy in your heart. If you try to serve the Lord by your strength, you will quickly burn out or find yourself serving with the wrong motives. You need to serve the Lord with these keys in mind so that your service will actually be a spiritual act of worship to God.

With His participation:
- *"For we are God's fellow workers; you are God's field, God's building." I Corinthians 3:9*
- *"If anyone speaks, he should do it as one speaking the very words of God. If anyone serves, he should do it with the strength God provides, so that in all things God may be praised through Jesus Christ. To Him be the glory and the power for ever and ever. Amen." I Peter 4:11*

With a willingness in your heart:
- *"We loved you so much that we were delighted to share with you not only the gospel of God but our lives as well, because you had become dear to us." I Thessalonians 2:8*

With a desire to see the completion of the service that the Lord has called you to:
- *"I have brought You glory on earth by completing the work You gave Me to do." John 17:4*

With humility in your heart:
- *"And being found in appearance as a man, He humbled Himself and became obedient to death – even death on a cross!" Philippians 2:8*

With the assurance that you will reap with joy the fruits of your labor:
- *"Those who sow in tears will reap with songs of joy." Psalm 126:5*

God calls me to be a fellow _____ with Him in the field of life. I can expect to serve in a labor that will sometimes produce _____, but I can be confident in expecting to reap with songs of _____.

When you apply the above noted keys to your acts of love (which is service to the Lord Jesus Christ), you will be able to overcome the temptation to serve with selfish ambition in mind (Galatians 5:13). Remember whom it is that you are serving and that His rewards will far outweigh anything you could possibly gain with selfish ambition. Serve the Lord with gladness and with a willing heart as He has commanded you to. Remember that God knows the hearts of everyone and he will reward (or punish) you for what you do (or do not do), so serve Him with the righteous He will provide as you seek Him in your life. Our God is a consuming fire Who will not be mocked.

> ☩ *"You, my brothers, were called to be free. But do not use your freedom to indulge the sinful nature; rather, serve one another in love." Galatians 5:13*
>
> ☩ *"Serve wholeheartedly, as if you were serving the Lord, not men, because you know that the Lord will reward everyone for whatever good he does, ..." Ephesians 6:7-8*
>
> ☩ *"Therefore, since we are receiving a kingdom that cannot be shaken, let us be thankful, and so worship God acceptably with reverence and awe, for our God is a consuming fire. Keep on loving each other as brothers." Hebrews 12:28-13:1*

I understand that God knows my heart; therefore, I should serve others in _____. I must serve _____ because the Lord will reward me for what I do. I commit myself to serving others in the area of _____ as the Lord has commanded me to do.

Life Application

If you truly have begun the application of the first eight principles to your life, you may begin to apply the principle of Christian service to your life. As always, this application begins with prayer, Bible study, and the counsel of other believers. Look at the burdens and talents the Lord has given you to begin serving His Kingdom. Begin with obtaining a sober estimate of yourself (Romans 12:3).

Burdens:			
Talents:			
Education:			
Day:	Prayer:	Bible Study:	Worship:	Fellowship:
Sun.		Psalm 23 Romans 12		
Mon.		Psalm 23 Romans 13		
Tues.		Psalm 23 I John 1		
Wed.		Psalm 23 I John 2		
Thur.		Psalm 23 I John 3		

Fri.		Psalm 23 I John 4	
Sat.		Psalm 23 I John 5	

Prayer:

_____
_____
_____
_____
_____

Worship:

_____
_____
_____
_____
_____

Fellowship:

_____
_____
_____

I confess that I need to increase my faith in Jesus Christ.

"And hope does not disappoint us, because God has poured out His love into our hearts by the Holy Spirit,

Increasing Your Faith in Jesus Christ

You must put your faith in the Living God because He is the One who gives life and blesses those that put their faith in Him (Matthew 9:29). Faith is being certain of an outcome or a confidence in someone or something without necessarily seeing immediate results or knowing immediate satisfaction. Faith is having the firm persuasion in your thinking that a statement is true and acting upon that thinking without doubting (II Thessalonians 2:13). Just as we may have faith that we will receive a paycheck at the end of the week or that our money is safe in the bank, we must put our faith in the truth and promises of our Lord Jesus Christ. Your faith in Jesus Christ is dependent upon the study of the Word, surrender to His will, and living a life that reflects that conviction. When you put these things, into practice, you will live a life that is pleasing to the

Lord and you will know His peace in your life (Isaiah 26:3). This peace and empowerment by the Holy Spirit will increase your faith as acting upon faith leads to a steady increase.

- ✞ *"Now faith is being sure of what we hope for and certain of what we do not see." Hebrews 11:1*
- ✞ *"But we ought always to thank God for you, brothers loved by the Lord, because from the beginning God chose you to be saved through the sanctifying work of the Spirit, and through the belief in the truth." II Thessalonians 2:13*

I confess that I have put my faith in _____ rather than God.

Faith comes from:

Faith is a gift from God and is part of His nature or character. God is always faithful to His promises even when we are not, because it is part of His divine nature to be faithful. Through His presence in your life, which is manifested in the presence of the Holy Spirit, you partake of His divine nature, which includes the ability to be faithful. By increasing the focus of your life to pleasing God and by increasing the amount you listen to His Word, you will harvest an increase of faith in your life.

- ✞ *"He is our Rock, His works are perfect, and all His ways are just. A faithful God who does no wrong, upright and just is He." Deuteronomy 32:4*
- ✞ *"For it is by grace you have been saved, through faith – and it is not from yourselves, it is the gift of God." Ephesians 2:8*
- ✞ *"Consequently, faith comes from hearing the message, and the message is heard through the word of Christ." Romans 10:17*

Faith is a _____ of God. I can increase my faith by listening to more of the _____ of God. I admit that I have listened to _____ rather than the Word of God.

How to activate your faith:

Faith comes from the Lord and needs to lead to an action on your part. The Bible is very specific that without an action on your part, your faith is not activated and therefore dead. True belief should lead to an action-filled life that shows the hope, trust, and confidence you have in the Lord. Let your actions reflect your hope, trust, and confidence in the Lord Jesus Christ. Putting your faith in Jesus Christ assures you success in conquering any life-controlling addiction and/or compulsive behavior. Christ assures believers victory in removing obstacles from their path (Mark 11:22) and purifying their life when their faith leads to obedience to Him. Your victory and purification is dependent on your obedience to the Lord's commandments, which is possible through His strength. A life of activated faith will lead to acts of righteousness and victory of the struggles of life. Further, a life of activated faith will lead you through the process of sanctification. Sanctification is the process that removes more and more of the sinful desires while replacing them with a life of righteousness through Jesus Christ. Obedience to the Lord will lead you through this process as He works out His good and perfect will in your life.

- *"In the same way, faith by itself, if it is not accompanied by action, is dead." James 2:17*
- *"He made no distinction between us and them, for He purified their hearts by faith." Acts 15:9*
- *"Therefore, we have been justified through faith, we have peace with God through our Lord Jesus Christ, through whom we have gained access by faith into this grace in which we now stand. And we rejoice in the hope of the glory of God." Romans 5:1-2*

Faith without action is _____! I declare that I must activate the faith God has given me by _____.

The results of activated faith:

Once you activate the faith God has given you and seek to purify your life through obedience to Him, you can begin to be pleasing to God. It is through faith and its actions that you are able to please God (Hebrews 11:6). Faith in Jesus leads you through the process of sanctification by which you may gain the fullness in Christ He gives to believers (Philippians 3:7-10) that live for Him and through Him. This process provides you with His strength so that you can do everything you are called to do (Mark 9:23).

- ☦ *"And without faith it is impossible to please God, because anyone who comes to Him must believe that He exists and that He rewards those that earnestly seek Him." Hebrews 11:6*
- ☦ *"Have faith in God, Jesus answered. I tell you the truth, if anyone says to this mountain, go, throw yourself into the sea, and does not doubt in his heart but believes that what he says will happen, it will happen, it will be done for him." Mark 11:22*

I confess that the mountain of _____ is still in my life because I have not put my faith in Jesus Christ.

Removal of idols

Faith in Jesus Christ must replace the faith you have had in the idols of your life. Therefore, you must repent of the idols you have treasured in your heart and put you faith in Jesus Christ. Remember that an idol can be a person or a thing that has become a god to you. Idolatry is defined worshipping something or someone other than God. It is someone or something that you honor, trust, serve, or go to as a replacement for the Lord. You must ask God to forgive you and repent from (turn away from) the idol in your life so that you can enjoy God's blessing in your life. Your faith in Christ will lead you to repentance as you begin to put your faith in the Word and desire to be obedient to it (Mark 1:15). This repentance begins the process of sanctification by which the believer begins to put their faith in the Word, which leads to a fuller life in Christ.

- ☦ *"This is what the Sovereign Lord says: Repent! Turn from your idols and renounce all your detestable practices!" Ezekiel 14:6*
- ☦ *"The time has come, He said. The Kingdom of God is near. Repent and believe the good news." Mark 1:15*

I confess that _____ has been an idol in my life. I now renounce this and ask Jesus to forgive me of that sin.

The fruit of faith in your life:

The fuller life in Christ enables the Christian to be victorious in spiritual warfare, which begins with protection from the enemy (I Thessalonians 5:8). The fruit of putting your faith in Christ manifests itself in hope, joy, peace, and confidence in Jesus. These fruits are yours to enjoy when you put your faith in Jesus and eagerly desire more. Recognize that God will always be faithful to do His part, therefore recognize that failure is the result in not doing your part. God has promised the Holy Spirit to those that believe and put their faith in Him, so that you can do your part. Continue to seek the Lord, act upon the faith He has already given you, and eagerly desire more faith so that you can continue to purify your life.

- *"May the God of hope fill you with all joy and peace as you trust in Him, so that you may overflow with hope by the power of the Holy Spirit." Romans 15:13*
- *"See, I lay a stone in Zion, a chosen and precious cornerstone, and the one who trusts in Him will never be put to shame." I Peter 2:6*
- *"The apostles said to the Lord, "Increase our faith!" Luke 17:5*

Hope by the power of the _____ leads to joy and peace. I declare that I will put my trust in the Lord Jesus Christ, because His hope never disappoints us.

Life Application

Merely reading the word of God and failing to apply it to your life is at best foolishness (James 1:22-25). You must apply the Living Word to your life if you intend to truly be a disciple of Jesus Christ (John 14:15). Pray, read, and write out a plan (Proverbs 29:18) for **applying** the word to your life beginning today! Each of four life essentials discussed in the introduction and found in Acts 2 need to be a part of your life. Keeping a journal of your prayer life, study of God's word, who you are having Christian fellowship with, and how you are applying your learning will begin the process of living a transformed life.

	Bible Study	Prayer	Worship	Fellowship
Sunday				
Monday				
Tuesday				
Wednesday				
Thursday				

Friday				
Saturday				

A Daily Evaluation of My Walk with Jesus Christ

I confess that I need to evaluate my daily walk with the Lord in the light of His word.
"Your Word is a lamp to my feet and a light for my path." Psalm 119:105

The reason you need to evaluate your daily walk is to ensure that you **continue** in your spiritual growth, which is evidenced in the development of Christian character. There is a tremendous danger in getting comfortable in your current level of Christian character because just as stagnation in a river leads to pollution and death so does stagnation in Christian character lead to worldly pollution and spiritual death. By examining your walk with the Lord, you can catch yourself before you fall into the traps of sin, which come through **complacency**. You need to depend on the Holy Spirit's leading and searching of your heart to guide you into the truth of your daily walk because your sin nature will deceive you if left to its own devices. Growth in Christian character is possible through the Lord as you replace a dependency on His creation with a dependency on the Creator. You should examine your Christian walk as you examine your development of Christian character (II Peter 1:2-11). The following passages of Scripture provide a checklist of Christian character traits while explaining where the power comes from for continued growth.

✞ *"Grace and peace be multiplied to you in the knowledge of God and of Jesus our Lord; seeing that His divine power has granted to us everything pertaining to life and godliness, through the true knowledge of Him who called us by His own glory and excellence." I Peter 1:2-3*

I confess that I have not partaken of the nature of Jesus Christ because I have relied on _____ to overcome my trials and temptations in life.

The previous passage of Scripture gives you guidelines for maturing in your walk with the Lord. The overall picture you can glean from this passage is that as you rely on God to lead you - He will give you the ability to mature in your Christian walk. It is His divine nature that you can partake of and His power that will enable you to grow in Christ-like character.

This process begins with knowledge of the Lord as verse two indicates. The knowledge referred to in this context is more than head knowledge – it is a knowledge that is **<u>relational.</u>** That is, it is a knowledge that comes from participation with the Lord in what He wants to do in your life. This relational based knowledge will exert a strong influence on your life that will enable you to develop. A key component in this relational knowledge is being obedient to His Word as the Scripture below indicates.

- ✞ *"If you abide in My word, then truly you are disciples of Mine; and you shall know the truth, and the truth shall make you free." John 8:31b-32*

God has enabled you to partake in His divine nature through the Holy Spirit, which then will eliminate your participation in the desires of the flesh or sinful nature. This process is one of continued change into the likeness of Christ (II Corinthians 3:18), which means you can mature in your ability to love God and others. You are capable of achieving this goal through your trust and obedience to the Lord. He puts His Spirit within you so that you can change and become new in the Him (II Corinthians 5:17).

- ✞ *"Therefore, if anyone is in Christ, he is a new creation; the old has gone, the new has come!" II Corinthians 5:17*
- ✞ *"And we, who with unveiled faces all reflect the Lord's glory, are being transformed into the likeness with ever-increasing glory, which comes from the Lord, who is the Spirit." II Corinthians 3:18*

I am completely a new creation in Christ when I surrender my life to Him. I declare that I have not surrendered the _____ of my life to the Lordship of Jesus Christ. I renounce this sin and ask Jesus to forgive me and make this area of my life new in Him.

The Lord has supplied all that you need to mature in your walk with Him - it is a choice to fulfill the call God has on your life, which will cause you to mature in your Christian walk. You are to endeavor to add the Christ-like characteristics listed in verses five through seven in order to fulfill the call and avoid the temptation of sin. Your faith should be exhibited in your actions (James 2:17). This action should include moral excellence, which is pleasing to God. When you add to this an experiential knowledge of the Lord, you are then able to add self-control (verse 5-6). Self-control enables you to persevere over the sinful nature (Romans 6:12). Perseverance refers to patience that is long-suffering and has the hope that will not surrender to circumstances (Hebrews 10:36). When you have added the patience to your walk with the Lord you are then able to add brotherly kindness, which is the brotherly love Christians are commanded to exhibit to each other (Colossians 3:12). Finally, as you have continued your spiritual growth you can add the love that comes from God, which is *"agape"* (in the Greek language) love. That is a love, which does not seek its own good, but rather seeks to give the target person what is best for that person regardless of the cost to the one giving the love. God exemplified this type of love in His sending Jesus to die for your sins (Romans 5:8). It was a love that was a complete sacrifice to the One giving it.

> ✝ *For by these He has granted to us His precious and magnificent promises, in order that by them you might become partakers of the divine nature, having escaped the corruption that is in the world by lust. For this very reason also, applying all diligence, in your faith supply moral excellence, and in your moral excellence, knowledge; and in your knowledge, self-control, and in your self-control, perseverance, and in your perseverance, godliness; and in your godliness, brotherly kindness; and in your brotherly kindness, love. For if these qualities are yours and are increasing, they render you neither useless nor unfruitful in the true knowledge of our Lord Jesus Christ. For*

he who lacks these qualities is blind or shortsighted, having forgotten his purification from his former sins. Therefore, brethren, be all the more diligent to make certain about His calling and choosing you; for as long as you practice these things, you will never stumble; for in this way the entrance into the eternal kingdom of our Lord and Savior Jesus Christ will be abundantly supplied to you." II Peter 1:4-11

If you are increasing these qualities in your walk, the Bible tells us that you will never stumble. Stumbling in this passage refers to falling away in sin, which is the opposite of the spiritual blessing promised if you continue to mature in your walk with the Lord. The spiritual blessing that comes out of this maturing includes joy (Psalm 36:8), grace to do what you should (II Corinthians 9:8), and the power to do more than you imagine (Ephesians 3:20). These qualities or character traits are available to you as you truly surrender your life to Jesus Christ and choose to put on the character that is available through partaking of the divine nature of Christ.

- ☦ *"And God is able to make all grace abound to you, so that in all things at all times, having all you need, you will abound in every good work." II Corinthians 9:8*
- ☦ *"Now to Him who is able to do immeasurably more than all we ask or imagine, according to His power that is at work within us," Ephesians 3:20*

I admit that I have allowed my sin nature to reign in my life and cause me to stumble as evidenced in my _____. I repent of this sinfulness and ask God to forgive me right now. I believe that God's word is true and declare that He is able to make all grace abound to me. He promises to give _____ I need to do the work He has given me to do. I believe His _____ is able to do more than I ask or imagine (Ephesians 3:20). Praise the Lord for His strength and love that has set me free to do what I should do. I commit myself to growing a Christ-like character for the glory of God. Amen.

Life Application

The relationship you are now beginning to develop with the Lord must include a daily evaluation. This evaluation must be based on the leading of the Holy Spirit and the application of God's Word to your life. Prayer and the accountability of fellow believers will round out the balance needed to truthfully evaluate your daily walk.

- ✞ *"Search me, O God, and know my heart; test me and know my anxious thoughts. See if there is any offensive way in me, and lead me in the everlasting ." Psalm 139:23-24*
- ✞ *"Blessed are those who hear the Word of God and obey it." Luke 11:28*
- ✞ *"Then you will call upon Me and come and pray to Me, and I will listen to you. You will seek Me and find Me when you seek Me with all of your heart. I will be found by you," declares the Lord, "and will bring you back from captivity." Jeremiah 29:12-14*

	Prayer	Bible Study	Worship	Fellowship
Sun.		Ephesians 6		
Mon.		Romans 8		
Tues.		Ephesians 1		

Wed.		Ephesians 2		
Thurs.		Ephesians 3		
Fri.		Ephesians 4		
Sat.		Ephesians 5		

Prayer:
_____
_____

Worship:
_____
_____

Fellowship:
_____
_____
_____

Appendix

> ☦ *For by these He has granted to us His precious and magnificent promises, in order that by them you might become partakers of the divine nature, having escaped the corruption that is in the world by lust. For this very reason also, applying all diligence, in your faith supply moral excellence,*

Define faith – Hebrews 11:1 "Now faith is the assurance of things hoped for, the conviction of things not seen."[1]

Define moral excellence- (Greek-Arête or pleasing to God as in virtue) and in your moral excellence, knowledge;

Define knowledge - an experientially knowing by participation with God

> ☦ *(6) and in your knowledge, self-control,*

Define self-control – temperance

and in your self-control, perseverance,

Define perseverance – patience or endurance through circumstances

and in your perseverance, godliness;

Define godliness – to worship well as in a real devotion to God

> ☦ *(7) and in your godliness, brotherly kindness;*

Define brotherly kindness – brotherly love that Christians are to have towards to one another and in your brotherly kindness, love

Define love – (Greek –Agape translated as charity or benevolent love, that is a love that does what is needed for the person).

---

[1] *The Revised Standard Version*, (New York: Oxford University Press, Inc.) 1973, 1977.

✝ *"For if these qualities are yours and are increasing, they render you neither useless nor unfruitful in the true knowledge of our Lord Jesus Christ. For he who lacks these qualities is blind or shortsighted, having forgotten his purification from his former sins. Therefore, brethren, be all the more diligent to make certain about His calling and choosing you; for as long as you practice these things, you will never stumble; for in this way the entrance into the eternal kingdom of our Lord and Savior Jesus Christ will be abundantly supplied to you." II Peter 1:4-11*

www.ingramcontent.com/pod-product-compliance
Lightning Source LLC
Chambersburg PA
CBHW080521110425
42742CB000173/3188